SHIT SHOW

An Unexpected Life
in Crisis and Risk Management

Matt Charles

Cover image © Shutterstock.com

www.innovativeinkpublishing.com
Send all inquiries to:
4050 Westmark Drive
Dubuque, IA 52004-1840

Contents

Part III: Self-preservation

Acknowledgments

I express my sincerest thanks to crisis and risk management professionals with whom I have worked throughout my career in law enforcement, academia, and communications. You have served your stakeholders well, sacrificing much.

The completion of this book would not have been possible without the counsel of Carole Sargent, PhD, Director of Scholarly Publications at Georgetown University; Kirk Schroder, Mike Keenan and the group at Schroder Davis; and the Innovative Ink team that includes Angela Lampe, Terri Nichols, and Lynne Rogers.

A special thanks to my friend and mentor, Karl Stauber, for taking a chance on me. My comms career would not have happened without you.

Finally, to my loving, encouraging, and beautiful wife, Melissa—the hardest working person I know—and our son, Cooper, the coolest person in the world. You two have been along for much of this crazy ride. Your support, advice, and understanding have helped me weather many storms.

To paraphrase Indiana Jones, "It's not the years, it's the mileage."

About the Author

MATT CHARLES is the former deputy spokesperson for the University of Virginia during and after the tragic Unite the Right rally in 2017 and many other crises. Prior to this position he served the UVA Darden School Business as Director of Media Relations, helping the school earn a #1 ranking through his reputation management work. A frequent media spokesperson, crisis and risk management professor, and former New York City special investigator working sex and drug crimes involving children, he has provided training for the U.S. Department of State and Drug Enforcement Administration, served on a working group for Washington, DC universities (Consortium 120) to combat gun violence and has received Fulbright support. Professor Charles provides strategic counsel for institutions of higher education, government organizations, nonprofits, corporations, and small businesses and startups. He teaches, or has taught, for Georgetown University, the University of Virginia, American University, Northeastern University, the University of Maryland Global Campus, the University of Iowa, Rutgers University, the University of Florida, the University of Alabama, and Purdue University.

Giovanni Cancemi/Shutterstock.com

Introduction

When I was a kid, I never would have thought I would enter a career in crisis and risk management. I wanted to be an FBI special agent or a Deputy U.S. Marshal (it turns out I always was great at tracking down people), working to protect our nation's people. Now that I look back, isn't that job ripe with crisis and risk management? Aren't many careers?

My approach to dealing with a crisis is simple—utilize perspective. With a background in law enforcement, I know well the difference between life and death. In most cases, I can walk into a room of frazzled individuals and remind them that no one died, so take a deep breath, and let's get to work. And if lives are lost, we need to work to protect others.

The more seasoned you are, the easier it is to contextualize, compartmentalize, and remove emotion from the equation. This being said, I do not mean to diminish the psychological, physical, and spiritual toll that dealing with crisis day in and out can take. In fact, I dedicate an entire class each semester in my crisis communication course to taking care of oneself when addressing a crisis. I also schedule a 15-minute period at the end of each class for students to share their crisis experiences from the previous week—catharsis is our friend.

The purpose of *Shit Show: An Unexpected Life in Crisis and Risk Management* is to provide crisis and risk management students and practitioners with the framework and tools to solve these life-altering events. Through easily digestible case studies that I have lived, you also will learn how to deal with something that people often do not speak—enduring disasters, emergencies, and calamities. Even the quickest and most fleeting of crises take a physical toll with increased adrenaline levels. For sustained crises, such as a natural disaster or an active shooter/shelter-in-place situation, one needs to guard against adrenal burnout. I have experienced these first-hand and watched colleagues—even the most experienced—succumb to them, at the least for a short period of time.

Crises seem to follow me in my professional and personal life. I guess that's why friends and colleagues have slapped me with the moniker—"shit magnet." One thing that I hold as a universal truth is that if it can happen it will, even the most unimaginable events. Thoughtful crisis preparedness and training help ensure that an organization can respond effectively when the inevitable occurs.

Stakeholders remember how a crisis was handled longer than the details of the crisis with organizations sustaining more long-term damage before and after a crisis than during the crisis itself (Herridge & Li, 2022). Proactive crisis communication helps minimize damage, improve morale, and encourages healing (Bowman & Schneider, 2021). The need for communication grows the longer the crisis continues, so one must prepare for a crisis to last days, if not longer.

The key to effective crisis management and communication is proactive planning. One must consider communication logistics. Do you have enough staff for coverage? Do you need to engage a crisis communication consultant?

We all know that a crisis can happen at any time, and that no matter how well one prepares and anticipates, a crisis can explode that no one thought or conceived possible. This being said, it is important to prepare as diligently as possible to help stave off a crisis (Coombs, 2007). This includes crisis plan preparation, the framework this chapter lays out.

PART I
How to Approach Crisis and Plan for Risk

Dilok Klaisataporn/Shutterstock.com

Crisis and Risk Management 101

The Call Comes In

Be it the 3 a.m. phone call from your CEO or president or a polite ask (even though we know it's not really an ask) to leave early from a vacation to return to work, a crisis can upend your life. If you are a crisis communication professional, you always know to be on the ready. But what if you don't have crisis experience, as is the case for many?

In a crisis situation, you will react as you are organized and trained (Machado & Anderson, 2022). Knowing what to do can draw the line between chaos and calm. The best practices and policies are only as effective as the organization that truly wants to be prepared and the people who implement them.

Stakeholders remember how a crisis was handled longer than the details of the crisis with organizations sustaining more long-term damage before and after a crisis than during the crisis itself (Herridge & Li, 2022). Proactive crisis management and communication help minimize damage, improve morale, and encourages healing (Bowman & Schneider, 2021). The need for communication grows the longer the crisis continues, so one must prepare for a crisis to last days, if not longer.

Both traditional media and social media have significant long-term impact on public perception and organizational reputation, but so do staff. So to the burning question—how do you prepare for a crisis?

As it pertains to crisis response, one must act quickly, but with factual information. Depending on the crisis, one must choose the appropriate spokesperson (Verčič et al., 2019).

When responding to a crisis, there are a few universal rules. First, lead with empathy to humanize the situation (Fannes & Claeys, 2023). Second, state what happened, that your organization will correct it, and what steps they will take to do so. Third, be as transparent as possible to foster credibility (Schoofs & Claeys, 2021). Sometimes, these corrective steps can position the organization as an industry leader, as it emerges from the crisis (Sellnow et al., 1998).

Crisis Preparation and Response

The key to effective crisis communication is proactive planning. One must consider communication logistics. Do you have enough staff for coverage? Do you need to engage a crisis communication consultant? If so, it is vital to bring them in before the crisis, so they understand your organization and a solid working relationship exists before things go south.

As it pertains to crisis response, one must act quickly, but with factual information. The crisis communicator does not act on speculation or hypotheticals. Once one has gathered the facts, compose a holding statement (Levick, 2020). Holding statements generally contain basic information to provide the media and other stakeholders and buy time to gain a deeper situational understanding and gather more information.

Other considerations are internal communication and spokesperson selection. Keep staff in the loop through internal communication tactics that can include email, town halls, and staff huddles (depending on organizational size). Internal stakeholders often are overlooked, which can harm staff morale—and thus—organizational effectiveness (Strandberg & Vigsø, 2016).

Depending on the crisis, one must choose the appropriate spokesperson (Verčič et al., 2019). For major crises, the chief executive must be front and center to convey the organization's serious attitude regarding the matter. The public information officer and chief communication officer or organization's designated spokesperson also must be available to triage and field media requests and relieve the chief executive in providing media updates. If technical expertise is necessary, for example, during an environmental disaster, subject matter experts can translate scientific or policy jargon and explain organizational response in layman's terms.

Risk Mitigation and Crisis Planning

We all know that a crisis can happen at any time, and that no matter how well one prepares and anticipates, a crisis can explode that no one thought or conceived possible. This being said, it is important to prepare as diligently as possible to help stave off a crisis (Coombs, 2007).

An effective method to do so is to conduct environmental scanning as part of one's daily issues management work. Environmental scanning is applied from systems theory where any and everything of which one may or may not be aware can potentially affect positively or negatively their organization (Slaughter, 1999). The Devil's Advocate Approach, which I introduce later in this chapter, stems from this idea. Issues management helps prevent and/or mitigate potential crises by catching them before they occur, which helps maintain reputation. If an issue looks like it will fester, it probably will—break the glass on your crisis management plan and prepare for crisis. Finally, continuously plan and evaluate so that one's organization remains on top of things to the best of their ability.

At the end of the day, no matter how prepared one might be for a crisis, surprises will happen. It's not an if—it's a when. However, with crisis communication planning one can better position themselves so that they are not caught completely off-guard and can spring into action.

The Devil's Advocate: Plan for Any and Everything

My experiences have provided me with a strong belief in rationality to mitigate and emerge from a crisis stronger than when one enters it. With time, a stronger conviction grew within me—the belief in The Devil's Advocate Approach. This process emerges from my conviction that anything and everything can happen at any time and one needs to be prepared for any variation.

In a nutshell, when crisis and risk management teams convene, one person will serve as The Devil's Advocate, proposing the most unbelievable outcome of a specified crisis, or a future crisis for which the team has no plan. Members should rotate through this role, but sometimes people are assigned The Devil's Advocate role more often due to their imagination and understanding of the sector in which they operate. I cannot claim to have invented this approach. Born from the Yom Kippur War, Israeli Military Intelligence has a Devil's Advocate Department Directorate Team. Prior to this, Winston Churchill used the approach before World War II when he predicted the rise of the German war machine when the vast majority believed the country could not rebound after its World War I defeat.

The Devil's Advocate approach is fundamental to successful enterprise risk management (ERM) communication. This practice helps avert crisis, but it also can aid in planning for crisis response.

Over the past 50 years, ERM has become increasingly important for leaders (McShane, 2018) with organizational leaders and their boards realizing the need for risk communication to support their crisis work (Reckelhoff-Dangel & Petersen, 2007). Recent examples that support this call-to-action include the COVID-19 pandemic, social justice movements, national security issues, geopolitical events, international financial systems collapse, legal issues, and cybersecurity breaches.

In leading organizations, crisis and risk communication professionals work hand-in-hand. A successful ERM practice helps prevent crises from occurring. On the other hand, if the risk becomes a reality, crisis communicators are there to help raise awareness about what happened, why, and what the organization will do to correct it. Like effective crisis communication, risk communication should be as transparent as possible and infused with empathy (Xie et al., 2021). ERM communicators and leaders can apply the following framework across sectors.

Risk Typology

Before exploring this framework, risk typology must be discussed. One must prepare for all challenges—no matter how conceivably improbable. If it can happen, it will, and the organization needs to be able to communicate about it. Here are the types of risk to monitor for:

- *Competition/Sector Risk*—states that competitors and an organization's respective sector constantly evolve, creating inherent possibility for peril.
- *Legal/Regulatory Risk*—recognizes that changes in laws and regulatory compliance can impact one's organization.
- *Organizationally Owned Risk*—comprises issues the organization may face from its own operations, management, and leadership that includes upset stakeholders; fraud, financial mismanagement, and impropriety; cybersecurity breaches; reputational damage; and poor product/service delivery and quality.
- *Social Responsibility Risk*—includes emergent social movements and changes that impact society and how the organization responds.

Enterprise Risk Management Communication Framework

Effective risk management requires risk identification, risk analysis, risk response, and risk monitoring. This framework allows organizations to plan accordingly for risk and know how to respond to it.

It is important to note that risk management differs from issues management in that risk management involves what could occur and how to prevent it, whereas issues management requires a response to stop an issue before it festers into a crisis (Compton et al., 2021).

Risk Identification necessitates spotting risks that could affect one's organization. Methods to do so include situation and SWOT analyses, environmental scanning, and competition/sector comparison (Schober, 2016). The ERM team, comprising stakeholders from throughout the organization, conducts this process. This teamwork helps to ensure that there are no blind spots with risks falling between organizational silos (Fra. Paleo, 2015). During risk identification, the team should appoint a "Devil's Advocate" to speak to why something could be a risk if others on the team do not think it could be. Remember—anything goes.

Risk Analysis and Impact requires the ERM team to chart how likely a risk is to occur. Part of this process requires working with stakeholders to gain insights regarding how they perceive the risk (Hoover et al., 2021). The risk communicator can conduct this primary research through quantitative research, such as surveys and questionnaires, and qualitative research including focus groups and interviews. The team assigns scores to each perceived risk—the highest score indicates the risk most likely to occur. After the ERM team scores the perceived risk, they assess the organizational impact (Soltanizadeh et al., 2016).

Risk Response involves how the organization will act on a risk once it becomes reality (Lee et al., 2009). Again, understanding how stakeholders want an organization to respond is essential. The risk communication professional crafts internal and external messages to disseminate to stakeholders regarding what occurred and how the organization will respond to the risk. Often, the crisis management team will help formulate and coordinate risk response.

Risk Monitoring requires watching potential risks and gauging how these perceived threats change (Hopkin, 2013). These shifts require ongoing evaluation to the risks' scores and how to respond to them.

Enterprise Risk Management Team Development is essential to help ensure that the organization is ready to address risk and communicate to stakeholders regarding it. Leading practice is to convene the team monthly to assess risk and modify their portfolio after evaluation. The ERM team also should act as part of twice-a-year crisis communication and emergency preparedness training led by an external facilitator. ERM, emergency preparedness, and crisis management plans should fold seamlessly into one another with team members' duties explicitly assigned. The facilitator conducts a debriefing after the meeting to determine what went well and what improvements the organization can make.

At the end of the day, ERM communication should advance organizational outcomes (Nair et al., 2014). One should not conduct risk communication simply for communication's sake. An added benefit is that this practice allows crisis and risk professionals to sit at the C-suite policy and decision-making table, boosting their importance within the organization.

PART II

Lessons from the Field

Nicholas Carty/Shutterstock.com

Catastrophic Loss of Industry in Rural Virginia

I knew in the ninth grade that I wanted a career in law enforcement, but I did not understand that community loss—including decimation of jobs—necessitated crisis management and communication. Maybe more importantly, risk management possibly could have prevented it—but, who knows, this was the 1990s when industry was collapsing left and right as the Early 1990s Recession took hold of the United States. Globalization was catching up with us.

The post–World War II boom saw net capital income average with 16–17% output and nonfarm labor productivity with a 2–2.5% growth from the 1950s through 1973 (Clark, 1984). These data points are mind-boggling, as they are, year after year.

With my hometown's loss of the iconic textile company Dan River Mills, Chapter 2 delves into what Danville, Virginia, could have done better from an economic development communications perspective and foreshadows my wife and my return to the city 13 years later—son on the way—to help spark its renaissance.

What Happened

At its apex, Danville, Virginia, was one of the most flourishing cities in Virginia. Started as the Wynne Falls ferry station, tobacco paved the way for Danville's 1793 charter. Over the course of the next century, tobacco merchants amassed a fortune, with the reality being many doing so through slave labor. From this group, six Danvillians founded Riverside Cotton Mills in 1882. This entity became Dan River, Inc.—the largest single-unit textile mill on the face of the Earth. In 1942, as the United States entered full-throttle into World War II after the December 1941 Japanese attack on Pearl Harbor in Hawaii, Dan River employed a staggering 14,000 out 40,000 Danville residents—35% of the population (Minchin, 2020). Just a few decades later the tide turned, as less expensive imported overseas textiles during the 1970s—coupled with a recession—caused Dan River to tumble into an irreversible slide.

My grandfather, and pretty much at least one family member of everyone I knew in town, worked for the Mill. My dad even had a short stint there in the 1960s after his military service before making the fortunate move of joining the U.S. Postal Service in the early 1970s. Many of my wife's family also worked there, including her paternal grandfather and grandmother.

This being said, the period in which I lived paled in success to earlier years when the desolate and vacant Downtown shopping district once thrived with a number of movie theaters, restaurants, hotels, and department stores. The black-and-white images from yesteryear truly seemed like ghosts—whispers from a distant past.

To be fair to international pressures that plagued Dan River until its demise, one can argue that its death nail was hammered when in the 1982–1983 period Wall Street investor Carl Icahn attempted to seize control (Lopez, 2013). Dan River's situation had been deteriorating for years. Icahn, with his mega-media presence and reputation as an investing genius who would buy businesses on the cheap and shudder them and sell them for parts at huge profits, just made it seem real.

The board, desperate to stave off Icahn, devised a spin-off corporation privately owned by employees that would buy Dan River. With high 1980s interest rates, the new corporation was saddled with a 125% debt-to-income ratio.

Once international competition became much stronger a decade later, Dan River was in the hole financially and a relic from an operational perspective, bereft of funds to bring it into the new millennium. These factors, coupled with drastically discounted textiles from Asia and Central America during the

1990s and early 2000s, dug a hole too deep to climb out of. A fabled giant that had survived the Great Depression of the 1930s eventually closed its doors in 2007.

The Impact and Response

When others have checked out due to self-pity or despair, occasionally a few will think ahead. Fortunately, for my hometown, this was the case. With the writing on the wall when Dan River was delisted from the New York Stock Exchange in January 2004 and filed for bankruptcy that March, compounded with the impending loss of Corning Glass among many other manufacturing jobs, a forward-thinking group began planning for the future. As Dan River's death was a slow-burn—a smoldering crisis in the truest sense—it was necessary to formulate a long-term play.

Their solution started quietly—in 2005, Danville Regional Foundation, or DRF, was incorporated in the Commonwealth of Virginia as a nonstock corporation (DRF, 2024). In my opinion, a smart move as once funds flowed in, they quickly could flow out to strategic targets to quickly strengthen the Danville area's health. This was the genesis of strategic philanthropy to the region that had become dependent on scattershot gifts and charity.

DRF was born of Danville Regional Medical Center's sale in 2006 and the subsequent $200 million endowment of its liquidated funds to DRF. It is important to note that DRF's service area is the Dan River Region, or the City of Danville, Virginia; Pittsylvania County, Virginia; and Caswell County, North Carolina—the original footprint of Danville Regional Medical Center.

Over the course of the next 18 years to date, DRF, with the help of community partners has reinvigorated not only Danville but also the Dan River region. DRF's intentional grantmaking centers around the four buckets of community development, economic development, education, and health and wellness. As of 2022, DRF had committed well over $100 million in grants and an endowment of almost $250 million, while transforming Downtown Danville, now the River District, into one of the most desirable places to live and helping the city earn its designation as a "Top 10 Digital City" for several years running—not too shabby.

What Could Have Been Done Better

To identify what the Dan River Region could have done differently to mitigate this crisis, we identify the risk types and then apply the Enterprise Risk Management (ERM) Communication framework:

Risk Identification

The City of Danville and the greater Dan River Region had the cards stacked against them as they faced Competition/Sector Risk, Legal/Regulatory Risk, and Organizationally Owned Risk with each strengthening the other through their entanglement.

Risk Analysis and Impact

- *Competition/Sector Risk*: Dan River's inability to modernize at the end of the 20th century hindered its ability to keep up with technological advances in the textile industry, thus allowing for an already bullish international market to undercut it through aggressive decreases in pricing. Without evolution, they didn't stand a chance.
- *Legal/Regulatory Risk*: Changes in federal laws and regulations opened a door for investors, like Carl Icahn, to come in and make a play. This ultimately forced Dan River's hand to restructure and take on a debt level that would squeeze the life out of the textile industry standard.
- *Organizationally Owned Risk*: Putting all their eggs in one basket from a manufacturing jobs perspective imposed a high level of risk. As Dan River faltered due to international competition pressures, inability to modernize, and debt from which they could not work their way out, hemorrhaging of jobs through layoffs and attrition were bound to occur with the textile titan's death an inevitability.

Risk Response and Monitoring

As these risks impacted and fed one another, it is best to address them as a synergistic entity. With Dan River's continued success, it was easy and understandable that they rested on their laurels regarding how they did business. It is important for the assigned Devil's Advocate, to remind the ERM team to acknowledge that history does repeat itself. Variables that include the actors and conditions under which they operate change the equation. This generally does not happen without a paradigm shift.

Having survived the Great Depression during the 1930s after a prosperous early 20th century should have informed Dan River executives and area leaders that the wartime and postwar boom of the 1940s and 1950s was not going to last forever. Diversification through myriad industries would have been prudent. With the locality's access to hydroelectric power and rail service, it would not have been a heavy lift to attract new businesses. Dan River could have used its capital and leveraged debt further to invest in ventures that were textile-related affiliate in nature or altogether different. This could have helped them put the infrastructure and financial capacity in place to give future corporate purchasers and overseas competition a fight.

Another consideration is that World War II quickly made the world a much smaller place, after which globalization likely was to occur. Preparing for this through looking outside domestic competition and identifying who could become an international threat could have changed Dan River's fate.

After identification of these risks, it is the duty of the ERM team to make constant evaluation and suggestion responses. Especially in a case like this where geopolitical events, labor issues, innovation, and corporate raiding likely could play a role, it is vital to monitor for changes in the tea leaves and shift accordingly.

Sabirov Nijaz/Shutterstock.com

The University of Virginia Balcony Final Exercises Collapse

On May 18, 1997, I attended the University of Virginia Final Exercises to support fraternity brothers and friends' graduation. About 10,000 others were crowded into UVA's Academical Village—a UNESCO World Heritage Site—on this morning. It is one of the most amazing a college graduate can experience as they process from the Rotunda down the Lawn to Old Cabell Hall.

However, that morning tragedy was to strike with a balcony collapse on one of the Pavilions that line the Lawn. As a second-year student, I had no idea of the UVA and local emergency and first responder personnel that would have to mobilize just 15 minutes prior to the ceremony where thousands of students had to walk past the scene. Twenty years later, I would have a much clearer picture when I served my alma mater as deputy spokesperson during the tragic events of August 11th and 12th, 2017.

What Happened

There are ten Pavilions on the UVA Lawn—many with accessible balconies—that house esteemed faculty and staff members. Between these Pavilions are Lawn rooms where fourth-year students live. Selection is based upon their merits, accomplishments, and contributions to the University and society. On the morning of Final Exercises, guests can ascend to the balconies for a bird's-eye view of the festivities.

From my vantage point at Pavilion II to the left of the historic Rotunda, I had a clear view of the Pavilion I balcony collapse that killed one and injured 18 with five of the injured being from the same family as the person who died. With my focus on the Rotunda waiting for graduating friends to appear in the caps and gowns, I heard a loud commotion across the Lawn and saw the balcony had given way. Part of it was suspended with people scrambling to get off before the rest of it, and those unable to evacuate in time, crashed to the ground.

Having passed inspection three years previously, there was no obvious indication of it failing. An investigation into the buildings' materials revealed the culprit—a corroded, iron rod supporting the balcony veranda (Allen, 1997).

The Impact and Response

Immediately following the collapse, UVA was slow to respond due to the lack of information and ability for an emergency preparedness team to coordinate immediately. This was before cellphones and operations team members monitoring laptops where they could initiate a call or Zoom at the drop of the hat to better understand in real-time what was happening from the vantage points of people on the ground.

UVA and the Commonwealth of Virginia restricted access to the balconies until further inspection took place with the mandate eventually being that no one could step onto the balconies until, out of an abundance of caution, all rods were replaced.

In a very different time before our current 24/7 communication connectivity environment, immediate access to information via social media and the Internet was not available. I, and probably many others, knew something serious had happened through first-hand observation or word-of-mouth, but before that evening's six o'clock news, we did not know the severity.

What Could Have Been Done Better

To identify what the University of Virginia could have done differently to mitigate this crisis, we employ the risk types and apply the Enterprise Risk Management (ERM) Communication framework:

Risk Identification

Even though the balcony was within its inspection period, UVA faced Organizationally Owned Risk. Given the unique and rustic building materials used in the Thomas Jefferson–designed structures erected in the early 1800s, more nuanced inspection was required. They also needed to address the lack of immediate communication to inform those in attendance and other stakeholders regarding what had happened.

With only minor injuries that include heat exhaustion and sprained ankles at previous Final Exercise events, there was no UVA Hospital medical designee at the command post to arrange for emergency transportation. However, their efforts would have been futile, as a metal chain fence obstructed access.

Risk Analysis and Impact

- *Organizationally Owned Risk*: UVA and the Commonwealth of Virginia realized the safety need to shut down the balconies immediately until the cause was identified and rectified. UVA would employ more historical preservation architects and archaeological teams to better ensure that older-construction buildings met guidelines. The event also helped inform future emergency preparedness plans where team members could assemble at the drop of a hat.

Risk Response and Monitoring

UVA Facilities Management instituted more regular inspections to better ensure safety. UVA Emergency Management created processes to assemble the appropriate parties quickly, disseminate information, and work to make sure events like this do not happen again.

Regarding the ERM team's assigned Devil's Advocate, they should have suggested worse-case scenarios that include major injury and/or death. This would have allowed for operations professionals, including a designated medical professional, to walk the graduation route and its periphery to ensure that all access points were open. In addition to meticulously checking structures along the graduation route for their soundness, regular security checks were needed to prevent dangerous implements that include firearms from making their way into the event. However, we live in a different world in 2024—I doubt even routine security checks were in place in 1997.

Matt Charles, Manhattan, 2002.

My Work as an NYC Special Investigator: A Mother Trying to Get Her Child Back

As a New York City child protective specialist working sex and drug crimes involving children for the Administration for Children's Services (ACS) my special investigation duties that liaised with the New York City Police Department Special Victims Unit (NYPD SVU) yielded myriad high-stakes, crisis-laden cases. Fortunately, my service as a Chesterfield County, Virginia, police officer prepared me well. Law enforcement officials, especially first responders, understand the need to serve as their own risk evaluator. Much of this is through lived experience, though the recent availability of data helps.

During my brief tenure before having the opportunity to attend graduate school presented to me, I worked on some interesting cases that included my very first arrest—having to cuff a belligerent 7-foot-tall male who had passed out drunk in a convenience store bathroom during midnight shift. My training officer offered the wise words of guidance that simply were, "You're up." The man was so tall that when he swung wildly with a knife at me, I didn't have to duck—but he did knock my hat off. After a punch to the stomach that doubled him over and sobering up a bit, the man apologized. He thought I was somebody else with whom he had a negative encounter earlier that day. It was all good, just part of the game. This event taught me to be prepared for any situation, no matter how unpredictable. I mean, come on, my first arrest being this?

Another memorable case was receiving the assignment in role call to collar a fugitive on the U.S. Marshal's Top Ten area list. Upon entering the residence where he was seeking shelter and—shocker—being told he wasn't there, we searched the premises. As I entered the bathroom, I saw boxer-clad legs dangling inside from a shower window. I pulled the man down and handed him off to the Deputy U.S. Marshal on-scene. Another lesson learned—trust, but verify. Both cases demonstrate the need for a Devil's Advocate to question and be prepared for what may come.

One NYC case that resonates most with me involved a mother recovering from crack addiction working through bureaucratic inertia to get her daughter out of the foster system. Little did I know after being assigned to the case that there also was an institutionalized brother that the father was exploiting for government money. She had done her part, and I felt deeply that I had to get these two kids back to their mother. This case delves into how the resolution of a crisis that blurs the lines of law enforcement and social work can advance an agency's credibility.

What Happened

Reviewing the case file upon receipt, it seemed pretty normal—a mother who had worked very hard to correct her ways was navigating the system to again live with her daughter under the same roof. However, this case would prove anything is possible and constantly would be in mind.

This one resonates not for the action like a case where a father hopped up on heroin jammed a knife to my throat. He knew I was there to remove his children, as both the father and mother had failed yet another drug test. To make matters worse, they had warning and knew when they had to take it.

Blade to my Adam's apple, I quickly flashed a smile and told him there must be a misunderstanding and that he didn't want to do this. I knew he cared for his child and wouldn't want them to see this. Seeing a glimmer of hesitation in his eye, I immediately knocked the knife from his hand and slammed his head into the sturdy pre-War construction sink. Cases like this are where the police training that judges loved and the social workers hated paid off, making sure I came home after a shift. During a hearing a few days later, his wife trailed me to the elevator. She told me that "I was a worthless piece of shit who only wanted to take their kids away from people." I asked her how the drug treatment was going. As the elevator door shut, she spit on me.

Hard to get scenarios like that out of your head. But this case was different for a number of reasons.

While in prison for drug charges, the mother had overcome a crack addiction that resulted in the removal of her daughter from her care five years before. The daughter was assigned to foster care. When we first met, we discussed the recovery work she had done and was continuing to do, as well as her plan to care for her daughter. It wasn't until I was leaving that she mentioned her son, who was not in the file. She didn't know where he was. Further investigation revealed that the father with whom the son lived and from whom the mother was divorced fabricated a mental illness to institutionalize the child to collect government subsidies while she was in prison. The son did have a learning difference that manifested at times as antisocial behavior, but nothing to warrant permanent hospitalization. Though the mother was ready to sue everyone involved with the situation, her sole focus was on getting her children back.

The Impact and Response

This case was a true multiagency effort. Through ACS I was able to locate quickly the daughter and commence regular visits with mother. The NYC Department of Health helped me find the hospital where the son was committed. Hospital officials did not have records of the father visiting the son—he had abandoned him and simply was collecting checks for being his biological father. Working with NYPD SVU, we tracked down the father, who later admitted to child abuse and fraud.

One attorney contested the child abuse charge, instead arguing for endangering the welfare of a child. This was absolutely crazy. After ACS legal counsel and I pointed to New York State Code Section 411-428 (New York Social Services Law, 2024) that states child abuse constitutes any injury inflicted intentionally, causing impairment of physical or mental health, disfigurement, death, or creating a high risk of injury or sexual abuse, the judge sided with us that mental toll taken on the son constituted child abuse.

With the mother continuing her recovery efforts, securing stable employment and becoming a strong antidrug voice and community advocate for ACS, she was granted the right for the daughter to live with her. The son joined them soon after. Seeing the family in the neighborhood at a later time, they appeared happy and healthy. Needless to say, the father went to prison and did not have access to the family.

What Could Have Been Done Better

As we have done throughout this book, we employ the Enterprise Risk Management (ERM) Communication framework to examine what could have done differently to mitigate this crisis:

Risk Identification

Even though the mother's actions warranted removal of the children, the fact that the son and the daughter were not mentioned together in the case file made it easy for him to disappear into the system and was exacerbated by the father's malicious actions.

Risk Analysis and Impact

- *Legal/Regulatory Risk*: The NYC Health Department was at risk for a lawsuit for not conducting deeper due diligence into the son's condition and trusting the father's reasons for having him institutionalized. After the case there were rumblings of a settlement, but I never learned if it came to fruition.
- *Organizationally Owned Risk*: ACS was at risk in that the initial investigation when the daughter was removed five years prior was not thorough, with the records reflecting this. After several incarnations and the 1995 murder of a child, ACS was formed through Mayoral Executive Order in 1996 with the focus to provide children and family the resources they needed through a sole agency, separate from the NYC Human Resources Administration. During the course of my time at the agency in the early to mid-2000s and after, ACS focused on providing the training needed for successful investigations, partnering with the NYC Department of Education to increase learning opportunities and focusing on placing children with families and away from residential care.

Risk Response and Monitoring

As stated in the "Organizationally Owned Risk" section, ACS did the work to better ensure the health and safety of the lives of the children who their mission was to protect. These reforms were based on leading practices at similar agencies and scholarly social work research and data analysis. Work also was done to advance information-sharing between city and state agencies that included improved technology and appointed liaisons.

Regarding the ERM team's assigned Devil's Advocate, I believe this case was bigger than just an ACS crisis—it was a bureaucratic maelstrom that could happen anywhere, but was especially possible in a city as large as New York where children can slip through the cracks. The Devil's Advocate could have suggested pressure-testing to locate systemic holes and interstate wide audits to determine whether unknown connections exist between families.

Jannis Tobias Werner/Shutterstock.com

2003 Blackout

It was Thursday, August 14th, 2003. I was trying to squeeze in a late afternoon case meeting in The Bronx before my parents drove into Manhattan from Atlantic City. Riding the 6 Train, I received a call that it was rescheduled. In those days, cellular signals underground were few and far between. Fortunately, I was able to receive this call above ground. I exited before reaching this outer borough and made my way to the train heading back toward my field office on 125th Street. Immediately, after logging onto my desktop, the building's power faded in and out. After a minute, it went dead. The landlines reverberated with busy signals.

With 9/11 less than two years in the past, our minds immediately went to another terrorist attack. Quick investigation showed that similar outages were occurring in a contiguous manner throughout the U.S. Northeast and Midwest and parts of Canada. Was this a terrorist act against our power grid infrastructure? With my parents driving into Manhattan and pregnant cousin on the Long Island Railroad on her way into the City for a family meet-up, I scrambled for answers.

What Happened

As I made my way down 125th Street toward the A train, it was immediately clear that New York City was at a standstill—traffic was gridlocked and subways were down due to lack of power. One of my colleagues, who had been working a case in the neighborhood, stepped across the street. Both of us feared the worst, but had no idea what was happening. There were no explosions or obvious signs of attack, but we knew that power and technological infrastructure could easily be taken down. The most amazing outcome to me, and this should not have been surprising, was how quickly New Yorkers rallied to help one another. Folks handed out bottled water and ice cream. Gelato shop owners passed out free scoops. People broke out flashlights and candles. That evening New York City felt like a nighttime festival.

As far as my family, I walked 54 blocks to my wife and apartment on W. 71st Street and Central Park West. From there I walked to my parents' hotel in Midtown. Fortunately, they had parked about an hour before the blackout. Another plus was that they had not had the time to deposit all of their Atlantic City winnings in the hotel safe, so had cash. It would take another 24–48 hours for ATMs and debit and credit card machines to come back online.

The Impact and Response

Fortunately this was not a terrorist incident, but the fact that the 2003 Blackout was reportedly caused by either a transmission line's contact with a tree or a brush fire did not mean that significant damages did not occur. Soon after, another transmission line failed, resulting in a cascade of failing lines. Over 50 million Americans lost power with an estimated $10 billion in economic losses. Most devastating, a 2012 article from the journal, *Epidemiology*, found that this crisis event resulted in approximately 90 more deaths than would normally have occurred during that couple-day span.

It is interesting to note that unlike many blackouts or other loss of infrastructure crisis events, criminal activity that includes burglaries, robberies, vandalism, and looting did not increase significantly. During the 1977 New York City Blackout crime skyrocketed. This was not surprising given that New York City was gripped by crippling poverty due to a financial crisis—just two years earlier the City was hours from declaring bankruptcy. To make matters worse during this blackout some 25 years earlier, residents were held psychologically hostage by the Son of Sam murders.

My personal assessment, and that of those who lived in the City during both blackouts, point to 9/11 ingraining a sense of care in residents for their fellow

New Yorkers. I can attest that we took care of one another during the 2003 Blackout. With subways down about a day-and-a-half and fire and EMT staff being called in extremely high volume, people stepped up to help neighbors in need. I witnessed two folks in my neighborhood who required medical assistance being carried down several flights of stairs by their hallmates to meet EMTs to help cut down on response times.

Regarding the power infrastructure, protective equipment was installed to better ensure an event like this did not occur again. Internal communications networks between power providers also were strengthened to better ensure exchange of information in real-time.

What Could Have Been Done Better

To better understand this case, we again employ the Enterprise Risk Management (ERM) Communication framework to examine what energy providers could have done differently to help make sure an event like this does not happen again:

Risk Identification

Power infrastructures require constant upgrades to avoid operational mishaps and terrorist attacks. Authorities that oversee these grids must make certain state, regional, and federal funds find their way to achieve this upkeep.

Risk Analysis and Impact

- *Competition/Sector Risk*: Solar energy has been a rival to traditional electrical power since the 1980s. However, given technological advances to make solar power more affordable, accessible, and effective and the introduction of robust tax credits, this energy source is a direct threat. Making the transition to solar even more compelling is that a case like the 2003 Blackout would have little chance of happening. The one caveat being large-scale solar power farms that are at-risk from weather events that include tornados and terrorist attacks. These considerations serve as threats to the power grid impact in 2003. In today's world, wind power turbines face similar issues.

Risk Response and Monitoring

Power authorities immediately responded with improved software, infrastructure pressure-testing, better internal communication and between agencies, and staff training. Risk monitoring included real-time system tests both from technological and physical perspectives and work to better ensure that international and domestic terrorists cannot infiltrate the grid.

As it pertains to the ERM team's assigned Devil's Advocate, talking with staffers soon after the 2003 Blackout this is one that some saw coming. The software was in need of updates with the result being that systems in place to alert staff of issues did not work. In essence, this crisis event was happening right in front of those tasked with protecting it—they had no idea until the lights went off.

The Devil's Advocate could have suggested that systems could fail with what was happening physically on-the-ground not matching with alarm systems. Camera systems, similarly to what we have with Ring technology, could help staff watch what actually is happening. Extrapolating to today's world, landlines to augment cell service should be available for staff to contact one another should cell towers go down.

My Introduction to Crisis Management and Communication:
A Dual Crime Scene with a Child Fatality and NY1 Reporter Struck by a Vehicle

September 19th, 2003, was a Friday and I was looking forward to the weekend.

I had worked three months straight with no days off due to taking leave for the wedding of my wife, Melissa, and I at our alma mater—the University of Virginia—on May 31st, 2003, and honeymoon to Jamaica. Needless to say, I was looking forward to a few days off. The summer of 2003 was crowded with violent, gut-wrenching cases, not to mention the 2003 Blackout that engulfed the U.S. Northeast and Midwest and parts of Canada.

rblfmr/Shutterstock.com

At the NYPD 26th Precinct with my SVU liaison on another case after a morning field visit, I was alerted to a reported child fatality around W. 120th Street and St. Nicholas Avenue. A sanitation truck had spotted a deceased infant deposited in the garbage about an hour earlier. Upon arriving at the scene, an infant's arm was exposed—the umbilical cord was still attached.

That afternoon, as we continued our assessment of the crime scene, muffled shrieks pierced our ears. To us, this sound means trouble, the kind of trouble that brings on immediate shock and awe. In our case, given the fact that we were investigating a child fatality, it was a scenario we would not have imagined— NY1 reporter, Rebecca Spitz, had been struck by a vehicle, fracturing her skull.

What Happened

While my focus and that of a NYPD SVU detective lasered on the dead baby NYC sanitation workers found, NY1 reporter Rebecca Spitz was struck by a vehicle as she crossed the street. She suffered a severe head injury. We had not one, but two, crime scenes. Given the child fatality, ACS was point. We did not have a public information officer available, so my supervisor asked me to handle media while I was on site. Simply put they stated, "Matt, I've watched you in court, and you handle yourself well. Let's put that UVA degree to use with the media. Just do your best." This assignment altered my career path forever. It was no secret that this job was wearing on me and my wife was concerned about the traumas I brought home every night, not to mention my personal safety. I can count several times where my life was in jeopardy, but fortunately I was able to work my way out of them.

The Impact and Response

The impact and response in this case is not what one would expect, as public information officers were not made available to child protective specialists during cases. NYPD had them on staff and continues to make them available.

My ability to gather information and think quickly on my feet to discern it to the media paid off here. However, it is not our job to serve double duty. Fortunately for ACS, the public didn't learn that this resource was not available.

What Could Have Been Done Better

To better understand this case, we use the Enterprise Risk Management (ERM) Communication framework to examine what could have been done differently to mitigate or avoid this crisis:

Risk Identification

It is vital to have channels available to communicate information. In my opinion, ACS thought that they did not have to shoulder this responsibility and that other agencies, such as NYPD, would provide the resources to do so. All agencies must have a communications arm to engage with both internal and external stakeholders. While my primary duty was to the child who died, once the reporter was struck, this also became my, and our agency's, responsibility.

Risk Analysis and Impact

- *Organizationally Owned Risk*: This one is pretty simple—ACS needed a public information officer available to handle communications, so child protective specialists could do their job, which is to investigate. My estimation is that one primary and one deputy public information officer per borough would suffice staffing requirements.

Risk Response and Monitoring

My briefing did not alter ACS communications behavior, but it did change the way I thought about engaging with media. I always felt a deep need to connect with the community to resolve cases—no one likes a child abuser or pedophile. However, this case made me realize that I had to be cognizant of media, a lesson I passed on to trainees.

Regarding the ERM team's assigned Devil's Advocate, again an easy one. As law enforcement officials, we know that things can blow up at any moment. Multiple crime scenes are an inevitability, but agencies need to have the ability and infrastructure in place to communicate information to the public, especially in cases where the public is in danger. To my knowledge Ms. Spitz recovered and lives a happy and productive life.

Andy Dean Photography/Shutterstock.com

The 2008 Housing Crisis

The 2008 Housing Crisis is among the most macro cases in this book, with 3.1 million Americans filing for foreclosure. It felt as if everyone knew someone directly affected, if they weren't personally, as the 3.1 million figure translates to 1 in 54 homes (Christie, 2009). Even with the American Recovery and Reinvestment Act of 2009, also known as The Recovery Act, this crisis would drag on for years. At its ascribed end, 10 million people lost their homes (Shalby, 2018). The reason—subprime lending. This practice provided mortgages to those who otherwise would not have qualified, creating a ripple effect that spurred the Great Recession.

This crisis was personal for me. My wife and I had lived in Los Angeles since 2004, moving there from New York City. In January 2007, we purchased a condo in North Hollywood with no money down. New buyers cannot fathom this concept. Widespread no-money-down, interest-only mortgages should have been a red flag, but millions didn't flinch at trading free money for ever-growing debt in exchange for a piece of the American dream. Further compounding our financial situation was closing on a property in our hometown of Danville, Virginia, in November 2007, just months before the 2008 Housing Crisis gripped the United States. Like many, we paid our bills, but suffered the consequences of those who did not. Over the next couple years, U.S. early mornings financial news and late-night European and Asian market reports that would inform the following U.S. day's markets consumed me, as I tried to firmly grasp what was happening so we could navigate financial catastrophe.

What Happened

Prior to the Great Depression, home ownership in the United States was difficult to achieve. People had to pay down the full amount or put 30% or more down-payments for very short-term home loans. With President Franklin Delano Roosevelt's New Deal Federal Housing Administration (FHA) and GI Bill, home ownership became much easier during World War II and after (McArthur & Edelman, 2017).

With the thirst for homeownership ever-expanding and creation of endless financial and monetary tools quenching it, things came to a head in the 2000s with the introduction of subprime loans. Many financial institutions offered high-risk individuals mortgages with higher interest rates than normal for the prize of owning a home, as well as adjustable rate mortgages (ARM) whose interest rates would increase over time. As an aside, we were offered the adjustable rate loan, but dodged that bullet. As property values cooled, some homeowners stopped paying their mortgages as their homes were underwater. Subprime recipients were the first to do so—many decided to walk away from their homes as they felt they could not regain the equity.

Soon after, banks and other lending institutions that include credit unions, traditionally the safest and most trusted community financial organizations, put a halt on lending. This in turn halted businesses' ability to borrow capital to perform day-to-day tasks that include making payroll and paying rent or mortgages. What began as a housing market crisis quickly morphed into a global financial crisis that could have rivaled the Great Depression.

The Impact and Response

The 2008 Housing Crisis was the main factor that precipitated the Great Recession. While Federal Reserve monetary policy to lower interest rates slowly helped to improve homeownership, the damage had been done. Even though the Great Recovery economic stimulus package provided immediate assistance and relief for the masses, many of the Wall Street titans and banks that helped create this crisis profited. A wider wealth disparity between haves and have-nots already was cemented into the mortar of the U.S. society. Those who were able to weather the storm invested in devalued real estate that eventually would recover.

The 2020 coronavirus (COVID-19) pandemic only fueled matters, as business owners were able to gain access to lending programs that included almost 0% interest rates available through the U.S. Small Business Administration Economic Injury Disaster Loans (EIDL) and Paycheck Protection Program (PPP) forgivable loans. One can argue the social justice crisis that emerged in the early days of the pandemic was exacerbated in part by the events that stripped many of homeownership over a decade earlier.

Regarding my personal connection to this crisis, our LA home lost half of its value in about six months, but it felt like a week to us. As we know, crises can alter perception. The Danville property weathered the storm better, losing between 15 and 20% of its value, because it was located in an already economically depressed area. Who knew that real estate investing in worse-off areas could serve as a hedge? Of course, all real estate is unique, but in the long-run, the LA property recovered its original value within about five years, while the Danville property never did before we sold it.

What Could Have Been Done Better

To better understand this case, we employ the Enterprise Risk Management (ERM) Communication framework to dive into what lenders and government regulators could have done to mitigate the risk for a crisis that could have plunged the world into another Great Depression, or worse:

Risk Identification

The writing was on the wall in the early to mid-2000s. The 2000 Tech Crash that had depleted many folks' investment portfolios was fresh in their minds. But the allure of easy money created by the subprime lending financial instrument erased this memory and almost plummeted the world into another Great Depression that, possibly, could have surpassed it in severity and recovery ability.

As with most crises, there are a few who foresee it and whose warnings usually go ignored. A group of housing attorneys and advocates read the tea leaves earlier in the decade and speculated that the housing market could go belly-up (Zahn, 2023). According to 2006 Inside Mortgage Finance data, in 2001 subprime loans made up just 7% of mortgages (Inside Mortgage Finance, 2006). By 2006, that number had skyrocketed to 23%—a 228% increase in just five years.

Risk Analysis and Impact

Regarding the risk typology, the 2008 Housing Crisis bats four for four:

- *Competition/Sector Risk*: Competition across the banking sector for increased profits to please shareholders and demand on employees to make potentially distressed mortgages a reality helped fuel this fire. Countrywide Financial—who financed our LA mortgage—was a leader. To paint an accurate picture, it was not Countrywide that pushed the ARM on us, but mortgage lenders. The entire sector took a reputational hit.
- *Legal/Regulatory Risk*: Lax regulatory practices helped make this happen. I preface this statement, in that they were lax in retrospect. Sweeping changes in monetary policy and lending practices stemming from the Great Depression recovery paved the way for the 2008 Housing Crisis over 70 years later. The irony is not lost on me.
- *Organizationally Owned Risk*: Both subprime and traditional lenders ran the gamut of risk indicators on this one. In financial ruin, reputation management was the least of their worries. Entities such as Countrywide and Washington Mutual simply were fighting to stay alive. In 2008 on the brink of folding, Bank of America acquired Countrywide and JPMorgan Chase, Washington Mutual. I remember watching reports of this trickle out during an early-morning workout.
- *Social Responsibility Risk*: While some might have been aware of how their lending actions could negatively affect communities, I think most probably weren't, as they were focused on making money. However, this doesn't matter as the social justice and inequity issues we now face were made that much more harsh from this crisis.

Risk Response and Monitoring

As it pertains to the ERM team's assigned Devil's Advocate, it appears they already were in place. If only someone would have listened to the housing advocates and attorneys who foresaw it—other than the few who shorted mortgage-backed securities in the financial markets and earned hundreds of millions to over a billion dollars in doing so. Shorting was their long-term play.

Blocking a Uranium Mine in My Hometown

Moving back to my hometown of Danville, Virginia, after living in Los Angeles and New York City was a bit of a jolt. Originally, the plan was for our Danville home to serve as a home-base when visiting family. Coming from Los Angeles with a baby on the way, we planned to spend extended periods of time in Danville.

However, I had no idea that I would oversee strategic communications for a large nonprofit foundation tasked with coordinating efforts to help ensure that a uranium mine with a potential billions of dollar payout could not operate. Hell, to be frank, I had no idea there was a proposed uranium mine in the area

RHJPhtotos/Shutterstock.com

when we moved back. But, hey, surprises keep life interesting, right? At least that's how I like to live, which is why I love working crises.

What Happened

It's hard to believe, but during the energy crises of 1973 and 1979 people had to wait in line for hours to take their turn at the pump. As a toddler during the 1979 event, gas lines were still on Americans' minds in the 1980s. In response, scientists and politicians began the search for energy alternatives, so we were not dependent on oil from the Middle East with the thought being we were one major geopolitical event away from another energy crisis that could have loomed much larger than previous iterations. These events impacted the public so much, I remember the term "oil shock" being thrown around.

In 1982, Marline Uranium Corporation located over 30 million pounds of high-grade uranium valuing just over 1 billion dollars near Chatham, Virginia, just outside my hometown Danville, Virginia (Isikoff, 1982). However, the economics of uranium waned as prices dipped in the 1990s causing Marline to go out of business. By 2007, the fickle uranium market once again was on the rise and Virginia Uranium, Inc. was born. Their mission was to successfully lobby the Commonwealth of Virginia General Assembly to lift the uranium mining moratorium to bring to the surface an estimated $7 billion in revenues. A 2011 Chmura Economics & Analytics estimated viable revenues to top out at $3.5 billion—still a load of unfathomable wealth (Chmura Economics & Analytics, 2011). Those who had signed uranium mining leases for deposits on their land were ready to cash in.

In response to the discovery, the Commonwealth sought to buy time to better ensure that mining could be done safely. Also, in 1982, Title 45.1, Chapter 21 of the Code of Virginia was made law (Code of Virginia, 2023). This code provides oversight of uranium exploration "and also included a moratorium on uranium mining," requiring that a program to regulate mining be established by statute before the Commonwealth could accept uranium mining permit applications.

To put this time span into perspective—I was entering kindergarten during the discovery and had just started my Director of Communications and Public Relations role some 30 years later. The next year would see many developments in the face-off with mining or maintaining the moratorium.

The Impact and Response

As Danville (VA) Regional Foundation (DRF) Director of Communications and Public Relations, I was charged with leading communications efforts to shed light on the potential ramifications of uranium mining in the area, positive and negative whether or not it came to fruition. Part of this work included compiling and summarizing five independent environmental, social, and economic impact reports totaling over 15,000 pages on uranium mining in the Dan River Region into a standalone comparative broadsheet one-pager (DRF, 2011) with corresponding report citations.

Questions included:

- Who funded the study?
- Why was the study conducted?
- What are the positive and negative environmental and health impacts of uranium mining and milling?
- What are the positive and negative economic and social impacts of uranium mining and milling?
- Are there recommendations for best regulatory and monitoring practices regarding the Coles Hill mine and mill?
- How long are the Coles Hill mine and mill expected to operate?
- What are projected tax revenues for the state and local region during the life of the mine and mill?
- Are there uranium mines and mills in the United States, or internationally, with which to compare the proposed Coles Hill site?
- What is the final conclusion of the report?

The various conclusions pulled directly from the one-pager are as follows:

- *After extensive scientific and technical briefings, substantial public input, reviewing numerous documents, and extensive deliberations, the committee is convinced that the adoption and rigorous implementation of such practices would be necessary if uranium mining, processing, and reclamation were to be undertaken in the Commonwealth of Virginia. (p. 223)*
- *Overall, the proposed mine and mill present both potential risks and rewards to the study region. Rewards include approximately 700 jobs and an added $162 million to the region's economy each year for more than 20 years. Risks include both actual environmental risks and perceived risks that could hurt the region's reputation. Risks could be significantly reduced if appropriate*

investments are made in design, pollution control technologies, regulatory development and implementation, and ongoing commitments are made to frequent monitoring and transparent communication. (p. ES-34)

- *In the opinion of Chmura, the mining and milling operations would bring substantial and much needed economic benefit to Pittsylvania County, the immediate surrounding areas, and the state. (p. 6)*
- *Conclusions could be impacted depending on the variation in key parameters, such as dam height for the uranium tailings containment structure, sediment concentration in the tailings, radioactivity level, uranium content, solubility characteristics of radiological elements and uranium, and the particle-size distribution. (p. 221)*
- *Significant amounts of radioactivity concentrations occur with significant failure of containment structure. (p. 221)*
- *This paper offers recommendations to decision-makers and communities on measures that should be taken to protect the public welfare prior to the commencement of the project. Specifically, the paper discusses the importance of the baseline data collection and sufficient bonding. (p. 2)*
- *Actions recommended as the Virginia legislature considers lifting the uranium mining ban include emphasizing source water protection as a critical component of the drinking water treatment process and creating state regulations that are more region specific. (p. 72)*

To summarize the studies' findings, while the region could benefit from increased jobs and economic benefit, environmental and health risks, which included water pollution, were high. Local and state governments' appointed and elected officials reviewed this resource. Just as Virginia Uranium did, DRF utilized op-eds and third-party advocate endorsements through local, state, and national media publications.

I also leveraged experience honed in Los Angeles and New York City to produce, direct, and host a public-access informational monthly television show—"DRF Digest"—in collaboration with the City of Danville, Virginia. "Digest" promoted DRF's efforts to advance the region through education, economic development, health and wellness, and community development with its reach being about 45,000 local residents. The platform informed viewers about the public policy efforts and research studies' findings regarding uranium mining. State and national media picked up on this effort.

Ultimately, the Commonwealth of Virginia upheld the moratorium and ban against uranium mining citing uncertainty regarding the risk for environmental damage and harm to the safety and well-being of residents and people as far away as the Atlantic coast given the watershed. In 2019, the U.S. Supreme Court upheld Virginia's ban on uranium mining (Chung, 2019). In 2022, *Nuclear News* reported that Consolidated Uranium acquired Virginia Energy Resources that holds the rights to the Coles Hill uranium deposit (*Nuclear News*, 2022). As this is the largest unmined uranium deposit in the United States, the fight continues.

What Could Have Been Done Better

To analyze this case, we utilize the Enterprise Risk Management (ERM) Communication framework to dive into what Danville Regional Foundation and its allies did well to encourage the Commonwealth of Virginia to uphold the decades-old uranium mining moratorium and what it could have done better. This work most likely laid the groundwork support for the 2019 U.S. Supreme Court ruling.

Risk Identification

With the rising price of uranium in the late 2000s into the very early 2010s, it was no surprise that Virginia Uranium was going to make a major play to have the uranium mining moratorium lifted. This work included lobbying efforts and stakeholder outreach. Given DRF's recent position as the regional leader, the Foundation served as the convener of information-providing bodies from various schools of thought to help the Commonwealth make its decision.

Risk Analysis and Impact

Regarding the risk typology matrix, Legal/Regulatory, Organizationally Owned, and Social Responsibility Risks existed:

- *Legal/Regulatory Risk*: In this case, the 1982 Commonwealth of Virginia code mandating a program to regulate uranium mining via statute had already provided a buffer for mining not to be rushed into action and bought time to gather more information. The bottom line is that the rules were in place for all parties by which to play.

- *Organizationally Owned Risk*: With DRF serving as the clearinghouse for study comparison, it knew it was going to take much heat from uranium mining supporters. The Dan River Region was in the midst of a long and painful economic downtown and people wanted jobs. There were many who argued that the environmental risks that could manifest in the future were worth it—families needed to eat today. This being said, DRF's program areas that included education, economic development, community development, and health and wellness made their involvement necessary.
- *Social Responsibility Risk*: Environmental justice had been evolving in its current form since the 1970s. The first Earth Day in 1970 helped usher into reality the U.S. Environmental Protection Agency and Clear Air Act (U.S. Environmental Protection Agency, 2024). If nobody acted to counter the lifting of the uranium moratorium, the environmental impacts could have been disastrous had an accident occurred. In addition to air quality and the impacts to the local geography, the Coles Hill watershed drains toward the Atlantic Ocean and could affect millions of people (Lewis, 2010).

Risk Response and Monitoring

As it pertains to the ERM team's assigned Devil's Advocate, it again already existed in some form. Both advocates against uranium mining and those who simply wanted more research before putting into place a legal statute had been watching the prices of uranium surge and dip over the years and were ready to act.

The 2017 Unite the Right Rally

As University of Virginia deputy spokesperson during the tragic events of August 11th and 12th when Nazi and white supremacist groups descended upon Downtown Charlottesville and the University, I was part of a regional group meeting to plan for this and the Ku Klux Klan rally held Downtown in July 2017. I was also part of UVA's 24/7 emergency response team from 2015–18; writing and disseminating real-time communications to internal and external stakeholders, as well as liaising with UVA, City and County and Virginia State Police officials.

Kim Kelley-Wagner/Shutterstock.com

As an exercise I had a superior ask me and my boss to take five minutes to write down, independently, the UVA crises we had worked over the past few years. The point was to demonstrate the volume, as we did not have to refer to records and each had five to ten that the other hadn't listed. My tally was 37. Even with this experience in addition to my time as UVA Darden School of Business Director of Media Relations, DRF Director of Communications and Public Relations, NYC special investigator, and Chesterfield County, Virginia police officer, I had never seen anything like this. The closest to this weekend—especially the night of August 11th with the parade of lit tiki torches, punctuated by chants of hate—in appearance, sentiment, meaning, and tone would be rallies in Nazi Germany during World War II.

What Happened

In February 2017, the City of Charlottesville, voted 3-2 to remove the Robert E. Lee statue that stood in the city's Market Street Park. In June 2017, Council voted to rename the park Emancipation Park. In doing so, they officially joined the ever-growing effort around the United States to remove Confederate monuments and statues from public areas. Since the end of the Civil War a total of 830 existed—there most likely were more (SPLC, 2019).

Given the high-profile attention the City received, most likely because it was perceived as a liberal stronghold with the University of Virginia being there, Nazi and white supremacist groups started plans to make a statement of their own. Devil's Advocate analysis was that the July 2017 Ku Klux Klan rally could serve as a dress rehearsal for a much worse August 2017 event, as participants could get a feeling for security measures.

On the evening of August 11th, 2017, Downtown Charlottesville looked like a demilitarized zone. I live blocks from there so I walked the area to provide on-ground eyes for UVA officials. To personalize matters even more, my wife's performance education theater was holding their largest production of the year at The Downtown Mall's Paramount Theater.

Monitoring my phone from the rear seats, I received a text around 9 p.m. that an estimated 300 Nazi and white supremacists were chanting loudly while walking toward the University of Virginia Rotunda with tiki torches. They had gathered about 15 minutes earlier behind Memorial Gymnasium at UVA's

Nameless Field. My mind took me four months earlier to May 2017 when Richard B. Spencer organized a rally against removal of the Lee statue. On that night, they demonstrated relatively quietly by candlelight. Tonight they operated in full Nazi fashion—spewing messages of hate underneath the cover of large flames. This was a calculated move.

Earlier that afternoon, social media chatter surfaced that a large number of tiki torches were bought at a local store with intent to use them that night. All information pointed to the Lee statue Downtown being the destination. However, the information was false and their wrath now pointed to the University of Virginia, specifically the statue of Thomas Jefferson and the Lawn that served as the intellectual and social center of the University. I'll be frank on this one—protest, in this case, was a kind word protected by the U.S. Constitution's First Amendment. The actual language within the Constitution is "peaceable assembly." Even if violent acts had not broken out, this was an act of intimidation, and, in my mind, war. Nazi chants of "Blood and Soil," a harkening to the Nazi Fatherland, do not ring peaceable assembly to me.

I was instructed to head home to monitor the media and be ready to deploy to the UVA Incident Command Center. As more on-ground information trickled in, I was struck by the group's precision—they were organized in two-by-two formation. My law enforcement days informed me they were ready for a fight in addition to making a pseudo-military statement of power.

As a UVA grad who hates bullies, here's where things got interesting and made me proud. Chants that included, "You will not replace us. Jews will not replace us," gained volume as they approached. Approximately 30–35 students, alerted to the group's approach, gathered and stood strong at the base of the statue. I'm confident some of them did not like Thomas Jefferson due to his past as a slaveholder, but they joined here to defend their home.

The next morning was a flurry. After a few hours of sleep, I woke up to my young son not feeling well. Before reporting to the UVA Incident Command Center, my wife and I took him to an early-morning doctor's visit. After learning that he had bronchitis and picking up his meds, I made my way to work, arriving about 30 minutes early. Not surprisingly, folks were on edge, as word had reached us that Nazi and white supremacists protestors had entered Emancipation Park around 8 a.m. that morning, many openly armed. Armed counter-protestors also were on site. By late morning, constant back-and-forth yelling and pushing among the groups occurred. Tensions escalated beyond the boiling point with rocks being thrown and fights breaking out.

As soon as I learned of this, I had ran across UVA Grounds to inform University leaders attending other events (including a large admissions event with at least 50 prospective students accompanied by their parents), to advise that in the interest of safety, UVA needed to shut things down and evacuate. At 11:52 a.m., Governor Terry McAuliffe issued a State of Emergency. I, along with other UVA communicators, sent messages to UVA stakeholders with situation updates and to inform them that the Governor had issued the State of Emergency, closing UVA until further notice. This declaration solidified my recommendation and all events were canceled, and the university closed.

While Grounds were evacuated without incident, other UVA officials and I continued to work around the clock on Friday and Saturday, August 11th and 12th, and into Sunday, August 13th. In situations like this, perspective and calm are key. In almost all crisis situations, I have to remind senior leaders and other stakeholders to take a breath and remember that it's not a life or death situation. This time, it would become just that.

As the threat of a return of Nazi and white supremacists to Grounds waned, at 1:42 p.m., James Alex Fields Jr. drove a Dodge Charger on Fourth Street into a crowd of counter-protesters. The violent force threw bodies into the air and killed Heather Heyer, for whom this stretch of Fourth Street was later named. He injured 19 others, some very seriously.

After returning from the bathroom around 5 p.m., over the radio I heard of a helicopter crash off of U.S. Route 29. We knew that Virginia State Police (VSP) were monitoring the scene. Two hours later, around 7 p.m., VSP identified the helicopter as theirs. VSP Aviation Unit Commander, Lieutenant Jay Cullen, and Trooper-Pilot Berke Bates were killed in the crash.

The Impact and Response

Amongst the flurry of media inquiries coming in the afternoon of August 12th, I noticed quotes from President Donald Trump regarding the tragic events. One, reported by media outlets across the globe (Shear & Haberman, 2017), really sticks out:

> *I think there is blame on both sides. You had a group on one side that was bad. You had a group on the other side that was also very vio-*

*lent. Nobody wants to say that. I'll say it right now. I've condemned
neo-Nazis. I've condemned many different groups. Not all of those
people were neo-Nazis, believe me. Not all of those people were white
supremacists by any stretch.*

At that moment, I knew things had changed. With the election of President
Trump and his free-swinging rhetoric regarding hate groups, the flood gates
opened and people felt free to come out of the shadows. I believe statements
like these laid the groundwork for the January 6th, 2021, Insurrection and
Attack on the U.S. Capitol.

As far as my work, I knew this surely was a global event when, on August
13th, I received a media inquiry from a Zimbabwe newspaper. In the following
months, I fielded a high number of media calls from local, regional, and national media that included *The New York Times*, CNN, *The Los Angeles Times*,
The Chronicle of Higher Education, and *The Washington Post*, helped navigate a
deluge of Freedom of Information Act (FOIA) requests, and assisted with draft
revisions to UVA's operating policy to better protect its students, faculty, staff,
and Grounds going forward.

UVA also worked to include students and provide resources to help with their
recovery after these traumatic events. Current and prospective Jewish students, people of color, and others did not feel safe, so various UVA groups and
leadership worked hard to make them feel so. An example of its work was that
in Fall 2018 UVA achieved its highest enrollments—both African American
students and overall applications with our strongest class matriculating to date
with 352 African American students enrolling (up 34% since 2013) and 1,310
minority students enrolling (up 35% since 2013).

On the one-year anniversary in 2018, Governor Ralph Northam issued a pre-
emptive state of emergency for Charlottesville to clear the way for Commonwealth of Virginia law enforcement and operational resources to be on the
ready and available should they be needed.

What Could Have Been Done Better

The Hunton & Williams (2017) *Independent Review of the 2017 Protest Event in
Charlottesville, Virginia*, prepared by Timothy Heaphy, presented and analyzed

the tragic events of August 11th and 12th, 2017. As UVA deputy spokesperson, one of my responsibilities was to review this document. Amongst Heaphy's team's findings, the positive finding I agreed with was that the Charlottesville Fire Department and UVA Health System set forth operational plans that made it simple for rescue crews to provide aid to large numbers of injured attendees quickly after attack (p. 151). I did not agree that "Law enforcement planning and response was informed by thorough, accurate intelligence before and during the event" (p. 152), as day-off information from the white supremacist groups did not match how events transpired.

Risk Identification

As it pertains to things that did not go right, as a former law enforcement official, the key points I agree with are Charlottesville Police Department not providing adequate training for an event of this magnitude and in lack of intelligence-sharing with on-ground officers (p. 153) and the University of Virginia Police Department (UPD) not accepting offers for assistance on the night of August 11th, that ultimately fed the fire for August 12th events (p. 158). From a communications perspective, lack of unified command structure and shared communications channels hindered effectiveness (pp. 164–165).

My belief and experience is that law enforcement entities must separate those at conflict and protect people at all costs. The report also supports this assertion (pp. 159–160). I personally have had times where I was not specifically cleared to act, but did so because people were in danger. My thought process was—what's the use of having the power to protect if you don't use it? Again, I caught administrative heat on occasion, but judges—the actual law—always had my back.

Risk Analysis and Impact

As it pertains to the risk analysis framework we have employed throughout this text, Legal/Regulatory, Organizationally Owned, and Social Responsibility Risks were at play. As I've examined them in-depth in the previous paragraphs, I'll make this quick:

- *Legal/Regulatory Risk*: As with many institutions, they can play things too safe, which can become a risk. In this case, not being proactive enough puts people in danger.

- *Organizationally Owned Risk*: As explained during this case, the reputations of the City of Charlottesville, Charlottesville Police Department, and University of Virginia Police Department were damaged. It took policy improvements, leadership changes, and deep community engagement to help replenish goodwill and reputational health.
- *Social Responsibility Risk*: In addition to Legal/Regulatory Risk, the inability to protect people is a Social Responsibility Risk. Furthering matters, UVA leadership taking too long to acknowledge Nazism and white nationalists/supremacists—instead identifying them as alt-right—was a risk. Given the violent actions by the Nazis and white supremacists, UVA stating the right to assembly by both sides came across as trying to strike a balance.

Risk Response and Monitoring

Playing Devil's Advocate in this position, I'll say what I said in 2017—when Nazis and white supremacists offer intelligence, don't trust it. Use it, verify it, but do not trust it.

Phillip Fryman/Shutterstock.com

The 2020 Nashville Tornado

Visiting family in Nashville, Tennessee, in late February into early March 2020 just before the COVID-19 pandemic gripped the United States, my wife, son, and I had a front-row seat to the historic high-end EF3 tornado that destroyed the historic Germantown neighborhood. In fact, you could say we were on the playing field. The building in which our Airbnb was located was the only one left standing, and our condo one of the few not affected. Fortunately, I heard the emergency siren in the middle of the night and was able to wake up and move my family to a secured space.

What Happened

During the evening of March 2nd, 2020, my family was packing to depart Nashville the following morning to head back to Charlottesville, Virginia. We were wrapping up an excellent few days of hanging out with family. Calling it a night around 10 p.m., nothing seemed out of the ordinary. I cannot remember the exact time I awoke, but I think it was after midnight, probably around 1 a.m. or so CST.

I heard what I thought was a barge sounding its horn in the distance. The condo was positioned just off the Wolf River, and we had seen several barges and tugboats slowly making their way down the river during our stay. As I was about to drift off to sleep, the sound amplified and sounded more like alert sirens. I sprung out of bed and pulled back the curtain to see furious lighting and very heavy winds bending the trees. Looking at my phone, we were under a tornado warning and in the path of one due to strike the area in about 5 minutes.

Fortunately, the layout of the condo was conducive to sheltering during a tornado even though we did not have access to a basement. Two bedrooms were connected by a large central bathroom with no windows and tub—with some luck, this would do.

I woke my wife and asked her to go to sit in the tub, while I went to wake our son. As I entered his room, the noise of the wind intensified with the cliché noise of "It sounded like a freight train" permeating the air. Making my way to his bed, I peeked through the window to see the tornado rip a municipal power generator from the ground, illuminated in sparks and brief electrical fire. From Southside Virginia, I was used to tornado warnings, but had never experienced one so close. My son was fast asleep, and I had started to pick him up, but he woke up and we made our way to the tub. The tornado upon us and ears popping due to the drastic change in barometric pressure, I closed and locked both bathrooms doors and lunged into the tub, as the condo went dark. Sitting in pitch black, we weathered the event for several minutes and stayed there for about 15 minutes longer to make sure this high-powered tornado had passed. Exiting the bathroom into the bedroom closer to the river, search lights popped up, one after another. What we saw seemed unbelievable. Talking amongst ourselves, we seriously asked, "Had we just survived this?"

The Impact and Response

The bouncing lights traced a scene of pure carnage. Large boats were thrown on the riverbank and buildings were leveled. Then we heard distant voices getting progressively louder. A flashlight revealed people clinging to a wall-less half-bathroom of what was a third-story condo in the building to the left of ours. This half-bathroom had been a full-bathroom. Water spewed from pipes torn from where the shower once was. I asked my wife and son to stay in the apartment while I checked to see if I could help. Both wanted to see what they could do, but with him being an 11-year-old, my wife agreed she would stay with him, especially as the danger was magnified with downed power lines littering the area.

As I walked toward the building, fire, police, and rescue crews asked me and several others to stay clear to allow them room to quickly evacuate people from the building, as they didn't know if it would collapse or not. I handed out some blankets and water and headed back to the condo. After checking in with family and friends in the area, we settled into one of the beds to call it a night. Given our adrenaline, helicopters patrolling with spotlights and the constant alert siren, it took a while to doze off.

The next morning, we found that our car was not damaged, though several had debris littered on them. We also learned that the bridge about a quarter mile from the condo was the site of a homeless encampment. A couple of them told of clinging to bridge columns with their feet lifted off the ground, thinking they were going to be sucked into the tornado's vortex. It took a while to make our way out of a gutted Germantown. We passed the pizzeria we had frequented, but there was nothing there, wiped clean by the storm's wrath. As we made our way along Interstate 40, the tornado's path was clear in the dirt on both sides of the highway. Homes and cars littered the highway's sides.

Effective emergency communications helped save lives and mitigate confusion during this disaster that killed 25, injured 309, caused $1.607 billion in property damage, and left 70,000 without electricity (NCEI, 2020; Straglin et al., 2020; Sutton, 2020). As I witnessed that night, as in New York City during the 2003 Blackout, people come together to help one another when they need it most. A shining example of community was the NHL's Nashville Predators making their home and arena available for locals to get a hot meal and recovery resources.

What Could Have Been Done Better

Given that this case was an unpredictable weather event, I do not know how things could have gone better. I do know they certainly could have gone much worse.

Risk Identification

Emergency preparedness teams sent weather alerts via cellphones and sounded alert sirens. For those who had television or Wi-Fi, local weather teams and

The Weather Channel provided real-time, very-detailed updates. Fire, emergency, and police responded immediately and worked tirelessly to tend to the injured and provide survivors aid.

Risk Analysis and Impact

As it pertains to the risk analysis framework, Organizationally Owned and Social Responsibility Risks were at play:

- *Organizationally Owned Risk*: Local municipalities regularly convene their teams and partners for practical exercises to rehearse for events like this. Understanding thoroughly how their communications, operations, and responses teams, among others, had to perform mitigated further loss of life.
- *Social Responsibility Risk*: The City of Nashville and surrounding counties' preparation, in addition to aid from the State of Tennessee and U.S. Federal Emergency Management Administration in the days and months that followed, made an already extremely difficult event more manageable for those affected through provision of aid.

Risk Response and Monitoring

If there was a Devil's Advocate designee in this risk management team, they correctly called for government officials to be ready to provide help in the case of a high-intensity tornado. Given that tornadoes occur frequently in Tennessee, this was the responsible play.

The COVID-19 Pandemic and Overnight Rush for Online Learning

One-and-a-half weeks after the Nashville tornado, on March 13, 2020, the world as we knew it shut down. COVID-19 had been making its way across the globe for a couple months. I remember well a dinner at New York's Chautauqua Institution only a few days earlier where a friend had colleagues in South Korea that had been hit hard and was under shutdown and quarantine. Conversation floated on whether we were next. Then we received our answer. Outside a couple nursing homes, COVID-19's U.S. invasion was quiet at first, but then it impacted us so harshly it forced us to seclude ourselves indoors.

Driving back from New York to Virginia, on Thursday, March 12, 2020, I listened as the Atlantic Coast Conference canceled its postseason men's collegiate basketball tournament in the midst of the quarterfinal round. Things were changing and at light speed.

What Happened

We found ourselves in the midst of a public health crisis not experienced since the Spanish Flu over a century ago. Educational institutions had to rethink literally overnight how they were going to instruct students. Having already taught predominantly online for five years—within days after March 13th, 2020—I received emails from numerous universities to help them navigate the new world. In the case of the University of Virginia, where I taught in the School of Continuing and Professional Studies, the entire university looked to us to help their students graduate on time through reconfiguring curriculum.

Due to lack of in-person classes, some students were in danger of not graduating as a result of sudden lack of internships. I was recruited to propose, design, and teach two sections of a strategic communications course for the UVA College & Graduate School of Arts & Sciences with the intention that it would help students land jobs. My proposal was one of 15 accepted from over 200. Over the course of a week, I designed a class that would serve 25 to 50 students in each section and help them gain jobs in the public relations field.

Other schools I assisted were Georgetown University and Purdue University. With the emergence of COVID-19, I served on faculty emergency support teams to help transition professors to the online space, aiding four professors directly on a 24/7 basis over the next several days as they moved courses online.

The Impact and Response

Like many organizations scrambling to maintain business continuity at the very beginning of the COVID-19 pandemic, higher education was in the same boat. However, to be fair to the many challenges colleges and universities faced, they were more like cities. In addition to facilitating classes, they had to ensure the health and safety of their students, faculty, and staff. Leadership teams worked around the clock to help ensure that COVID-19 did not spread, and if it did, that their health providers could treat the infected.

While all the schools with which I am affiliated met the challenge, almost all of the thousands of higher education institutions did so, as well. Out of the gate, many students preferred online classes—COVID-19 just served as the change agent to alter the market in favor of this learning platform preference (Gallagher & Palmer, 2020). The interesting takeaway is that while some yearn to return to in-person learning, my experience is that many graduate students prefer—at least for now—the shift to asynchronous and synchronous learning modalities, as most work full-time and many have families. These learning formats more easily accommodate these lifestyles.

What Could Have Been Done Better

Risk Identification

Given that COVID-19 was a once-a-century pandemic event, from a higher education perspective, things went surprisingly well. This is especially true given that colleges and universities are known for their glacial-speed institutional inertia. As far as some nations' responses, that is a matter for another case study. Most schools were able to make a sharp pivot to online learning within a week. Information technology teams worked tirelessly to make this happen.

Risk Analysis and Impact

As it pertains to the risk analysis framework, Competition/Sector, Legal/Regulatory, Organizationally Owned, and Social Responsibility Risks were in motion:

- *Competition/Sector Risk*: Colleges and universities had to work to maintain the quality of their education rigor and keep them running. If they did not do so, others would be more than willing to accept transfer students to help increase revenue.

- *Legal/Regulatory Risk*: From a regulatory perspective, all bets were off. Higher education governing bodies realized that they would have to do whatever it took to keep students in class, while maintaining their health.
- *Organizationally Owned Risk*: Outside of well-being, schools were in danger of shuttering. They had to quickly and effectively shift to an online format in a smart financial manner. To foster goodwill, some schools issued room and board partial or full refunds, as students were not on-ground. Some also offered online courses at a discounted rate.
- *Social Responsibility Risk*: At the end of the day, colleges and universities had to keep people safe. Many did at a financial cost from which some still are digging their way out of the COVID-19 hole.

Risk Response and Monitoring

In this hopefully once-in-a-lifetime crisis event, the Devil's Advocate would pose to the team the scenario where an infectious disease completely wreaks havoc on business continuity. They could point to the 1918 Flu and various plagues as examples. Given ever-increasing populations and global travel, the likelihood of another pandemic event happening sooner than later is moderate to high.

The Salman Rushdie Assassination Attempt

The morning of August 12th, 2022, felt normal, but the day turned out to be anything but.

My wife planned to leave vacation a day early to get back to work. I was going to stick around and give my son and his friend a ride home the next day. As I drove her car to park it for packing, something felt off. I saw a couple people sprint past. My mind immediately went to the morning lecture speaker on the Chautauqua Institution Grounds that I looked forward to listening to after I

Markus Wissmann/Shutterstock.com

helped her. As soon as I exited the vehicle, I saw two people walking slowly, gazing forward in a state of shock.

In an instant, my gut told me what I would confirm a few minutes later. An armed visitor to Chautauqua, Hadi Mater, had rushed the stage and stabbed world-renowned author Salman Rushdie multiple times in the stomach and chest, inflicting critical injuries that would place him on a ventilator and cost him an eye. Fortunately, staff and audience members acted quickly to subdue and disarm Matar, who was acting on a 1989 fatwa that the Ayatollah Ruhollah Khomeini decreed after Rushdie's book, *The Satanic Verses*, hit the shelves that year.

How could this happen in such a sacred place that people have come for 150 years in search of revitalization and relaxation? The simple answer is it can happen anywhere.

People needed answers quickly to Rushdie's condition, whether Grounds were safe, what had transpired, and the status of Chautauqua operations going forward due to the lockdown.

A few minutes after hearing multiple witnesses say Rushdie had been attacked, an uneasy—but only too familiar—feeling flooded me. This was the fifth anniversary of Charlottesville, Virginia's, tragic events of August 11th and 12th (see Chapter 9), the city in which I live that still is recovering from that weekend.

I lived both events. One as a vacationer in the place where we seek renewal who wanted answers and the other as the deputy spokesperson for the University of Virginia in the city where my wife and I attended UVA during the late 1990s and the community we came back to raise our son where I had to help provide answers and information.

What Happened

After Rushdie had just had a seat on Chautauqua Amphitheater stage at 10:47 a.m. that Friday morning, Hadi Matar rushed the literary giant from behind and began stabbing him. An almost 4,000-person capacity audience, with hundreds standing outside the gates, watched in horror. Fortunately, Matar did not take into account that Chautauquans, even those in their retirement years, are people of action. Several jumped from their seats and climbed the stairs to the stage to assist staff members and law enforcement in subduing Matar. During this incident, moderator Ralph Henry Reese, also was injured, but released from the hospital later that day.

After being airlifted from Sharpe Field, Rushdie would spend the next six weeks in the hospital, part of it on a ventilator. He suffered ten stab wounds and liver damage and lost an eye and feeling in parts of his hands. At this point of my life, not much surprises me, but seeing images of the helicopter landing at a field on which I have played softball the past ten years made me take pause.

The Impact and Response

Within minutes rescue personnel quickly made their way on stage to attend to Rushdie. Chautauqua Institution evacuated the Amphitheater after Matar's apprehension and locked down Grounds within about an hour after the attack. My wife was one of the last people to exit the gates, as she was already on her way back to Charlottesville, Virginia.

Local, state, and federal law enforcement officials performed the initial phase of their investigation that included combing the Grounds and surrounding area for further threats, taking statements, and processing the crime scene. It is interesting to note that during this time, and within about 2 hours of the attack, the regional Critical Incident Stress Management team arrived to provide crisis counseling to first responders and those staying on Grounds (Bump, 2022). From my experience, this is an extremely rapid response time with the average time being two to three days after the crisis event.

As the world media watched, Chautauqua Institution President Michael E. Hill presided over an afternoon press conference to provide an overview of what happened and updates regarding what was known (Pilkington, 2022). He could not speak publicly about everything at that point. This is common practice as organizations cannot release all facts during a pending investigation, as not to jeopardize it. It was apparent that a security audit would occur with changes to precautions taken during events and accessibility to them.

What Could Have Been Done Better

As we have done throughout this book, we employ the Enterprise Risk Management (ERM) Communication framework to examine what could have been done differently to mitigate this crisis at a place some regarded one of the safest in the world:

Risk Identification

Salman Rushdie had been under the threat of fatwa since 1989, living under police protection for a while until shunning it to live a more normal life. I respect Rushdie's personal preferences, but as a former law enforcement official, his appearance was a high-risk incident across the organizationally owned risk. However, this incident could ignite legal and regulatory changes, as happened after the tragic events of August 11th and 12th in Charlottesville, Virginia (see Chapter 9).

Interestingly, Chautauqua's fierce dedication to open dialogue and providing honest conversations in an open and free space put it at organizationally owned risk. It is important to state the caveat that Rushdie officially owned his own risk by denying a personal security detail.

Risk Analysis and Impact

- *Organizationally Owned Risk*: Knowing Chautauqua's geographical layout (gated community on a lake) and its culture accustomed to extremely open accessibility (well-known speakers walk and interact freely with guests), I was impressed with Grounds being locked-down within about an hour. Another proactive action was that there was increased law enforcement presence for this event. However, given that an active assassination attempt was still out for Rushdie, several actions were needed.
  These included:
  1. More plain-clothes law enforcement in attendance during the event.
  2. An advance team to vet and correct security lapses and watch for people who might act maliciously.
  3. Stricter Grounds access that included shutting down lake access to those without verified identification.

4. Actionable command center to increase communication information-sharing and speed.

Risk Response and Monitoring

Chautauqua Institution instituted noticeably more security measures for the remainder of the 2022 Season that included more law enforcement personnel, increased identification verification to enter Grounds, and not allowing bags into some venues. During the off-season and before the 2023 Season they hired a Director of Organizational Safety and Security who was tasked with conducting a security audit in conjunction with a task force of local, state, and federal law enforcement officials and suggesting actionable safety plans to help ensure an event like this does not happen again (Ryan, 2023). In essence, the Institution hired someone to think strategically and oversee campus security, much like many colleges and universities have in place. This is leading practice, as places like these are most similar to cities where a lot can happen fast.

The director also implemented an updated opt-out emergency notification system for community alerts and emergency preparedness software so that Chautauqua staff can communicate in real-time should a crisis event occur. Regional law enforcement collaboration also increased with regular check-ins and coordination.

Regarding the ERM team's assigned Devil's Advocate, I would be surprised if the possibility of a Rushdie assassination attempt was not put forward. This being stated, it is an outcome for which they should have thoroughly prepared to prevent this horrendous act from occurring. From a reputational standpoint, Chautauqua Institution's security measures were questioned, but they took appropriate and thoughtful action to emerge from this crisis in a better state from safety, security and operations perspectives.

PART III

Self-preservation

Chanintorn.v/Shutterstock.com

Don't Let Your Mental Health Become a Casualty

This short chapter traditionally would be an afterword in some crisis and risk management texts, if included at all. However, its message is incredibly important and vital, as the need to preserve one's mental health is paramount to a career in this field. This resource is so treasured, that I dedicate an entire class each term to it and allow time weekly for students engaged in this work to talk through things, if they wish. The same goes for Executive Education classes I teach.

While one cannot control the events that put a crisis into place, one can control their response. Instead of becoming unhinged, one can maintain composure and calm. Besides the benefits of being able to think more clearly in this state, how can one expect to lead and maintain the respect of their staff and peers if they have lost it?

There is no magic or complexity to caring for oneself and their team during a crisis event. Just as those directly affected, the professionals working to help those involved and bring the crisis to a close are impacted. So what do we do to protect ourselves? While the answers are simple, taking the time to perform them, especially with little available time, is not so easy.

Usually, once a crisis takes form, dual teams will work 12-hour shifts. Of course, if things are really bad, it might be all hands-on deck for at least a couple days. Even if this is the case, one will take breaks in which they should disconnect for at least 15 to 30 minutes. During time away, it is important to exercise, drink plenty of water, and eat well. If one likes to read or watch TV to unwind, this can be productive to transport one's mind from the crisis. For the spiritual and religious, one can benefit from prayer or a visit to their local place of worship for a moment of quiet reflection and contemplation. All of us can benefit from quality engagement with family and friends.

One tool that some shy away from but I have found personally beneficial is counseling. Until a couple years ago, I never saw the need. After the COVID-19 lockdown, I worked with a therapist and found it most helpful. The interesting thing was that I wasn't seeking help for work, but realized its merits in all facets of my life. The bottom line is if you do not take care of yourself, you are not helpful to those in crisis. You also are not able to be fully present and attentive to yourself, family and friends.

Case in point, there was an event after my wife's birthday in October 2021 where she, my son, several of her staff, and I were walking back to our cars just off Charlottesville's Downtown Mall. As we laughed and talked, we heard the unmistakable sound of twisting metal. Looking to the right, a bus careened toward us. One of the group had seen the bus first and pushed my son out of its path. The rest of us followed.

Like a scene out of the movie, *Speed*, the bus came to rest on the sidewalk about ten yards away from us. Down the street was a damaged truck. While the staffer who first noticed the bus checked on its driver, I and another by-stander worked to get the truck's driver out of the vehicle, as we smelled gasoline. Fortunately, we were able to do so before rescue workers arrived.

The bottom line is that a regimen of self-care helps keep you sharp and on the ready for whatever life throws at you. There might come a time when you need to help those you love most in times of immediate crisis. You need to be there for them, too.

REFERENCES

Allen, Mike. 1997. "Snapped Rod Caused Fatal Balcony Fall." *The Washington Post* 5, no. 20.

Anderson, G. Brooke and Michelle L. Bell. 2012. "Impact of the August 2003 Power Outage on Mortality in New York, NY." *Epidemiology* 23, no. 2: 189–193.

Baruch College Zicklin School of Business. 2024. "New York City (NYC) Blackout of 2003." *NYC DATA*. Accessed February 15, 2024. https://www.baruch.cuny.edu/nycdata/disasters/blackouts-2003.html

Bowman, Courtney D., and Erika J. Schneider. 2021. "Finding an Antidote: Testing the Use of Proactive Crisis Strategies to Protect Organizations from Astroturf Attacks." *Public Relations Review* 47, no. 1: 102004–.

Bump, Alyssa. 2022. "CISM Team Responds to Chautauqua Community Following Salman Rushdie Attack." *The Chautauquan Daily* August 16. Accessed February 29, 2024. https://chqdaily.com/2022/08/cism-team-responds-to-chautauqua-community-following-salman-rushdie-attack/

Christie, Les. 2009. "Foreclosures up a Record 81% in 2008." *CNN Money* January 15. Accessed February 29, 2024. https://money.cnn.com/2009/01/29/real_estate/Hope_Now_foreclosures_easing/index.htm

Chmura Economics & Analytics. 2011. "The Socioeconomic Impact of Uranium Mining and Milling in the Chatham Labor Shed, Virginia." November 29. Accessed February 29, 2024. https://archives.bape.gouv.qc.ca/sections/mandats/uranium-enjeux/documents/ECON1-AN.pdf

Chung, Andrew. 2019. "Virginia Ban on Uranium Mining Upheld by U.S. Supreme Court." *Reuters* June 17. Accessed February 29, 2024. https://www.reuters.com/article/idUSKCN1TI1R4/

Clark, Peter K. 1984. "Productivity and Profits in the 1980s: Are They Really Improving?" with Discussants: Charles L. Schultze and Robert J. Gordon. Brookings Institute. *Brookings Papers on Economic Activity* no. 1: 133–181.

Code of Virginia. 2023. Title 45.1, Chapter 21. Accessed February 29, 2024. https://law.justia.com/codes/virginia/2021/title-45-1/

Compton, Josh, Shelley Wigley, and Sergei A. Samoilenko. 2021. "Inoculation Theory and Public Relations." *Public Relations Review* 47, no. 5: 102116.

Coombs, W. Timothy. 2007. *Ongoing Crisis Communication : Planning, Managing, and Responding.* 2nd ed. Los Angeles: SAGE.

Danville Regional Foundation. 2024. Accessed February 14, 2024. https://www.drfonline.org/

Danville Regional Foundation. 2011. Uranium Study Board. Accessed February 19, 2024. https://www.drfonline.org/content/drf/uploads/PDF/uranium-study-board-17.pdf

Fra.Paleo, Urbano. 2015. *Risk Governance The Articulation of Hazard, Politics and Ecology.* Ed. Urbano. Fra.Paleo. 1st ed. Dordrecht: Springer Netherlands.

Gallagher, Sean and Jason Palmer. 2020. The Pandemic Pushed Universities Online. The Change Was Long Overdue. *Harvard Business Review* September 29. Accessed February 18, 2024. https://hbr.org/2020/09/the-pandemic-pushed-universities-online-the-change-was-long-overdue

Herridge, Andrew S, and Xinyang Li. 2022. "Surfing for Answers: Understanding How Universities in the United States Utilized Websites in Response to COVID-19." *Journal of Comparative and International Higher Education* 14, no. 3B: 111–129. https://files.eric.ed.gov/fulltext/EJ1360232.pdf

Hoover, Anna G. et al. 2021. "Balancing Incomplete COVID-19 Evidence and Local Priorities: Risk Communication and Stakeholder Engagement Strategies for School Re-Opening." *Reviews on Environmental Health* 36, no. 1: 27–37.

Hopkin, Paul. 2013. *Risk Management.* 1st ed. Philadelphia, PA: Kogan Page.

Hunton & Williams. 2017. Independent Review of the 2017 Protest Events in Charlottesville, Virginia. Accessed February 29, 2024. https://www.policinginstitute.org/publication/independent-review-of-the-2017-protest-events-in-charlottesville-virginia/

Inside Mortgage Finance. 2006. *Funding for Mortgages Data Set.* Accessed February 17, 2024. https://www.insidemortgagefinance.com/

Isikoff, Michael. 1982. "Uranium Found In S. Virginia Tobacco Fields." *The Washington Post* July 21. Accessed February 29, 2024. https://www.washingtonpost.com/archive/politics/1982/07/22/uranium-found-in-s-virginia-tobacco-fields/980d12fb-1bce-4e0b-aa4a-32df46fe9ca3/

Lee, Ka Lok, Robert J. Meyer, and Eric T. Bradlow. 2009. "Analyzing Risk Response Dynamics on the Web: The Case of Hurricane Katrina." *Risk Analysis* 29, no. 12: 1779–1792.

Levick, Richard. 2020. "Cybersecurity in the Age of Cyber-Espionage, Nation-State Hacking, and Criminal Abundance." *Of Counsel* 39, no. 4: 5–20.

Lewis, Maggy. 2010. "Keeping Agriculture Alive in the Shadow of a Uranium Mine: Potential Effects and Regulatory Solutions for Virginia." *William & Mary Law and Policy Review* 34, no. 2: 615–652.

Lopez, Linette. 2013. "The Time Carl Icahn Fought an Entire Virginia Town and Lost." *Business Insider* 8, no. 7. August 7. Accessed February 29, 2024. https://www.businessinsider.com/carl-icahn-danville-virginiadan-river-2013-8

Machado, Sara A., and Patricia N. Anderson. 2022. "The Perspectives of Preschool Teachers Regarding Their Ability to Respond to Various Crises in the Childcare Center." *Journal of Early Childhood Research : ECR* 1476718.

McArthur, Colin and Sarah Edelman. 2017. "The 2008 Housing Crisis: Don't Blame Federal Housing Programs for Wall Street's Recklessness." *Cap 20* April 13.

McShane, Michael. 2018. "Enterprise Risk Management: History and a Design Science Proposal." *The Journal of Risk Finance* 19, no. 2: 137–153.

Minchin, Timothy. 2020. "Dan River Mills." In *Encyclopedia Virginia*. December 7. Accessed February 29, 2024. https://encyclopediavirginia.org/entries/dan-river-mills/

Nair, Anil et al. 2014. "Enterprise Risk Management as a Dynamic Capability: A Test of Its Effectiveness During a Crisis." *Managerial and decision Economics* 35, no. 8: 555–566.

National Centers for Environmental Information. 2020. *NCDC Tornado Summaries.* Accessed February 18, 2024. https://www.ncei.noaa.gov/access/monitoring/monthly-report/tornadoes/202013

New York State. *New York Social Services Law.* 2024. 411–428.

Nuclear News. 2022. "Virginia Uranium's New Owner Hopes to Wait Out Mining Moratorium." *Nuclear News* November 21. Accessed February 29, 2024. https://www.ans.org/news/article-4512/virginia-uraniums-new-owner-hopes-to-wait-out-mining-moratorium/

Pilkington, Ed. 2022. "Rushdie Attack Prompts Questions Over Security at New York Event." *The Guardian* August 13. Accessed February 29, 2024. https://www.theguardian.com/books/2022/aug/13/salman-rushdie-attack-security-chautauqua

Reckelhoff-Dangel, Christine, and Dan Petersen. 2007. *Risk Communication in Action: The Risk Communication Workbook.* Cincinnati, OH: United States Environmental Protection Agency, Office of Research and Development, National Risk Management Research Laboratory.

Ryan, Arden. 2023. "With Eye Toward Balancing Best Practices With Community Culture, Haubert and Department Share What to Expect." *The Chautauquan Daily* June 24. Accessed February 29, 2024. https://chqdaily.com/2023/06/with-eye-toward-balancing-best-practices-with-community-culture-haubert-and-department-share-what-to-expect/

Schober, Madrean. 2016. "Role and Practice Development." *Introduction to Advanced Nursing Practice* Cham: Springer International Publishing. 95–109.

Schoofs, Lieze, and An-Sofie Claeys. 2021. "Communicating Sadness: The Impact of Emotional Crisis Communication on the Organizational Post-Crisis Reputation." *Journal of Business Research* 130: 271–282.

Sellnow, Timothy L., Robert R. Ulmer, and Michelle Snider. 1998. "The Compatibility of Corrective Action in Organizational Crisis Communication." *Communication Quarterly* 46, no. 1: 60–74.

Shalby, Colleen. 2018. "The Financial Crisis Hit 10 Years Ago. For Some, It Feels Like Yesterday." *The Los Angeles Times* September 15. Accessed February 29, 2024. https://www.latimes.com/business/la-fi-financial-crisis-experiences-20180915-htmlstory.html

Shear, Michael D., and Maggie Haberman. 2017. "Trump Defends Initial Remarks on Charlottesville; Again Blames 'Both Sides.'" *The New York Times* August 15. Accessed February 29, 2024. https://www.nytimes.com/2017/08/15/us/politics/trump-press-conference-charlottesville.html

Slaughter, R. A. 1999. "A New Framework for Environmental Scanning." *Foresight* 1, no. 5: 441–451.

Soltanizadeh, Sara et al. 2016. "Business Strategy, Enterprise Risk Management and Organizational Performance." *Management Research Review* 39, no. 9: 1016–1033.

Southern Poverty Law Center. 2019. "Whose Heritage? Public Symbols of the Confederacy." *Southern Poverty Law Center* February 1. Accessed February 29, 2024. https://www.splcenter.org/20190201/whose-heritage-public-symbols-confederacy

Straglin, Doug, Ayrika L. Whitney, and Gentry Estes. 2020. "Pretty Much Like an Explosion: Day After Brutal Nashville Tornadoes That Killed 25 People, 3 Still Missing." *USA Today* March 3. Accessed February 18, 2024.

Strandberg, Julia Matilda, and Orla Vigsø. 2016. "Internal Crisis Communication: An Employee Perspective on Narrative, Culture, and Sensemaking." *Corporate Communications* 21, no. 1: 89–102.

Sutton, Caroline. 2020. "Here's What to Know About the Tornadoes That Killed 24 in Tennessee." *WTVF* March 3. Accessed February 18, 2024. https://www.newschannel5.com/news/seven-killed-in-middle-tennessee-storms-widespread-damage-reported

U.S. Environmental Protection Agency. 2024. "EPA History: Earth Day." https://www.epa.gov/history/epa-history-earth-day#:~:text=The%20First%20Earth%20Day%20in%20April%201970&text=Because%20there%20was%20no%20EPA,issue%20onto%20the%20national%20agenda

Verčič, Tkalac Ana, Dejan Verčič, and W. Timothy Coombs. 2019. "Convergence of Crisis Response Strategy and Source Credibility: Who Can You Trust?" *Journal of Contingencies and Crisis Management* 27, no. 1: 28–37.

Xie, Chaowu et al. 2021. "The Effects of Risk Message Frames on Post-Pandemic Travel Intentions: The Moderation of Empathy and Perceived Waiting Time." *Current Issues in Tourism* 24, no. 23: 3387–3406.

Zahn, Max. 2023. "Housing Advocates Forecasted the 2008 Financial Crisis, They Said They Were Ignored." *ABC News* October 21. Accessed February 29, 2024. https://abcnews.go.com/Business/housing-advocates-forecasted-2008-financial-crisis/story?id=103718982